Dear Santa,

CHRISTMAS Photos

CHRISTMAS DAY *Planner*

Morning

Afternoon

Evening

CHRISTMAS DAY *Memories*

My Favorite Memory	Highlight of the Day

CHRISTMAS WISH List

WHAT I'M HOPING FOR

THINGS I REALLY NEED

MY FAVORITE THINGS

CHRISTMAS *Journal*

CHRISTMAS Countdown

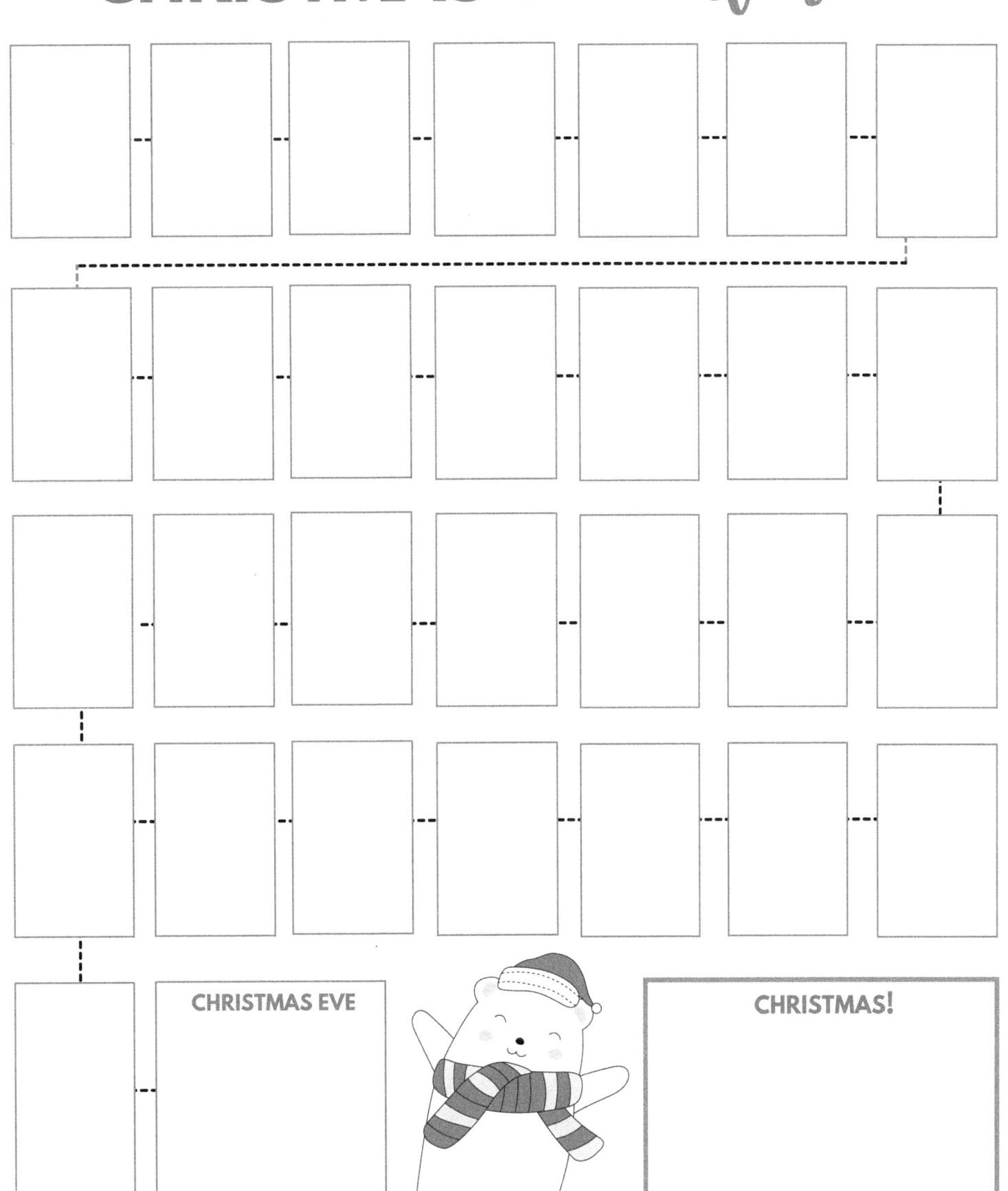

CHRISTMAS EVE

CHRISTMAS!

CHRISTMAS *Journal*

ONLINE SHOPPING *Tracker*

ITEM	WEBSITE	COST	RECEIVED?

NOTES & REMINDERS

CHRISTMAS *Journal*

CHRISTMAS SUPPLY *List*

CHRISTMAS GIFT *Ideas*

NAME: **BUDGET:**

GIFT IDEAS

NAME: **BUDGET:**

GIFT IDEAS

NAME: **BUDGET:**

GIFT IDEAS

NAME: **BUDGET:**

GIFT IDEAS

NOTES

CHRISTMAS PARTY *Planner*

LOCATION		DATE	

THEME	DRESS CODE	NOTES

SCHEDULE

TO DO LIST

ACTIVITIES / IDEAS

MEAL PLANNER

HOLIDAY WEEK *Schedule*

Day	Schedule
MON	
TUE	
WED	
THU	
FRI	
SAT	
SUN	

PRIORITIES

TO DO

NOTES

Décor PLANNER

THEME

BUDGET **ACTUAL COST**

IDEAS

SCHEDULE

COLOR SCHEME

THINGS TO BUY

NOTES

CHRISTMAS SHOPPING List

ITEM   PRICE   STORE

NOTES & REMINDERS

CHRISTMAS GIFT *Tracker*

NAME	GIFT	BOUGHT

CHRISTMAS CARD *Tracker*

RECIPIENT:
ADDRESS:

○ WRITTEN   ○ MAILED   ○ RECEIVED

RECIPIENT:
ADDRESS:

○ WRITTEN   ○ MAILED   ○ RECEIVED

RECIPIENT:
ADDRESS:

○ WRITTEN   ○ MAILED   ○ RECEIVED

RECIPIENT:
ADDRESS:

○ WRITTEN   ○ MAILED   ○ RECEIVED

RECIPIENT:
ADDRESS:

○ WRITTEN   ○ MAILED   ○ RECEIVED

CHRISTMAS PARTY *Invites*

NAME	CONTACT INFORMATION	RSVP'D

CHRISTMAS BUDGET *Tracker*

TOTAL BUDGET GOAL	ACTUAL COST

NAME	BUDGET	GIFT PURCHASED	AMOUNT SPENT

CHRISTMAS GIFT *Tracker*

NAME OF STORE	ITEM TO PURCHASE	COST

ELF ON THE SHELF *Ideas*

SUPPLY LIST

OTHER IDEAS

 # CHRISTMAS COOKIE *Recipe*

RECIPE NAME:

Category: **Source:** **Prep Time:**

Temperature: **Cook Time:** **Serves:**

INGREDIENTS

DIRECTIONS

NOTES

HOLIDAY *Recipes*

SERVES: **PREP TIME:** **BAKE TIME:**

Ingredients

Instructions

CHRISTMAS *Journal*

CHRISTMAS *Journal*

Dear Santa,

CHRISTMAS Photos

CHRISTMAS DAY *Planner*

Morning

Afternoon

Evening

CHRISTMAS DAY *Memories*

My Favorite Memory

Highlight of the Day

CHRISTMAS WISH List

WHAT I'M HOPING FOR

THINGS I REALLY NEED

MY FAVORITE THINGS

CHRISTMAS *Journal*

CHRISTMAS Countdown

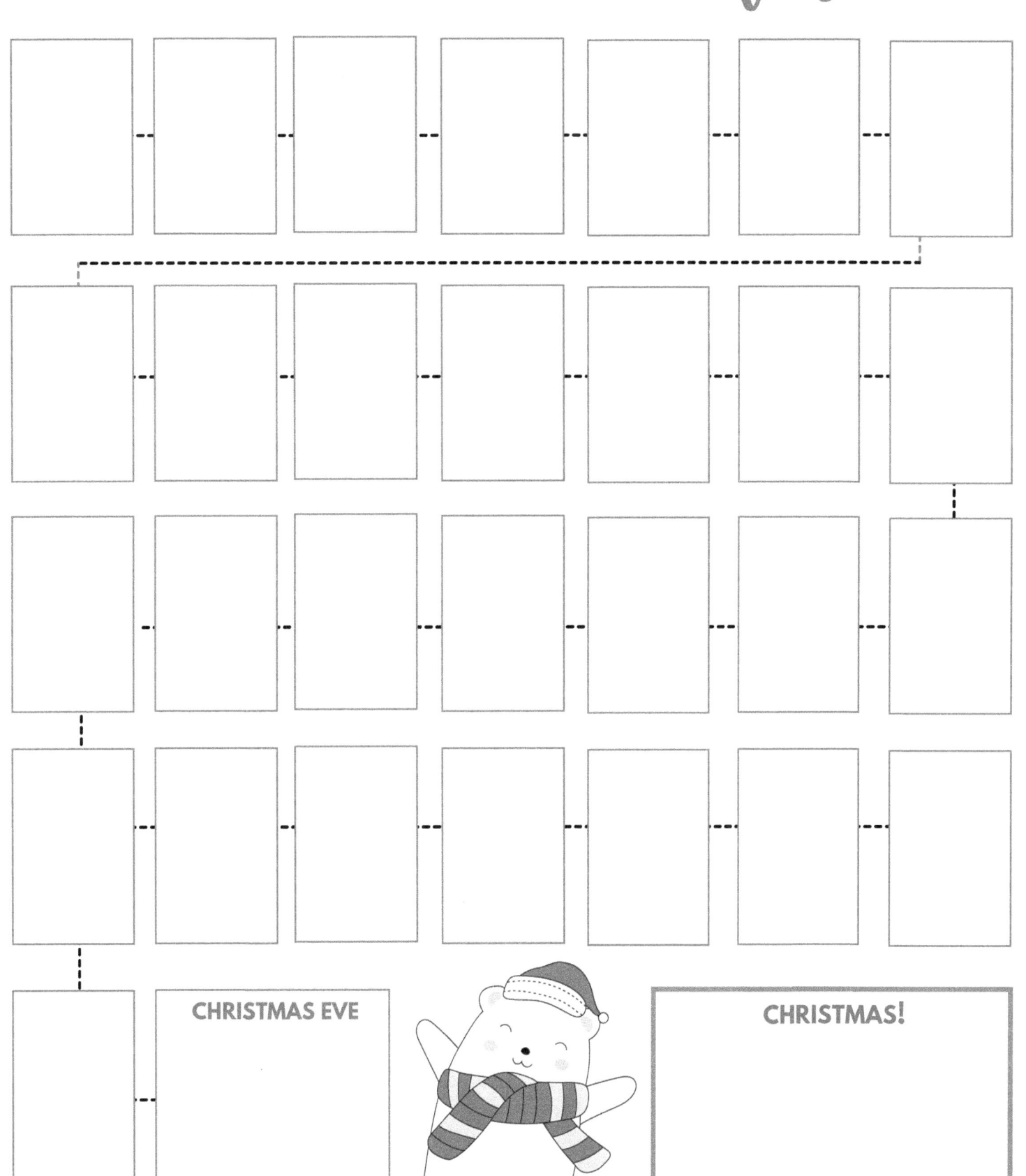

CHRISTMAS EVE

CHRISTMAS!

CHRISTMAS *Journal*

ONLINE SHOPPING *Tracker*

ITEM	WEBSITE	COST	RECEIVED?

NOTES & REMINDERS

CHRISTMAS *Journal*

CHRISTMAS SUPPLY List

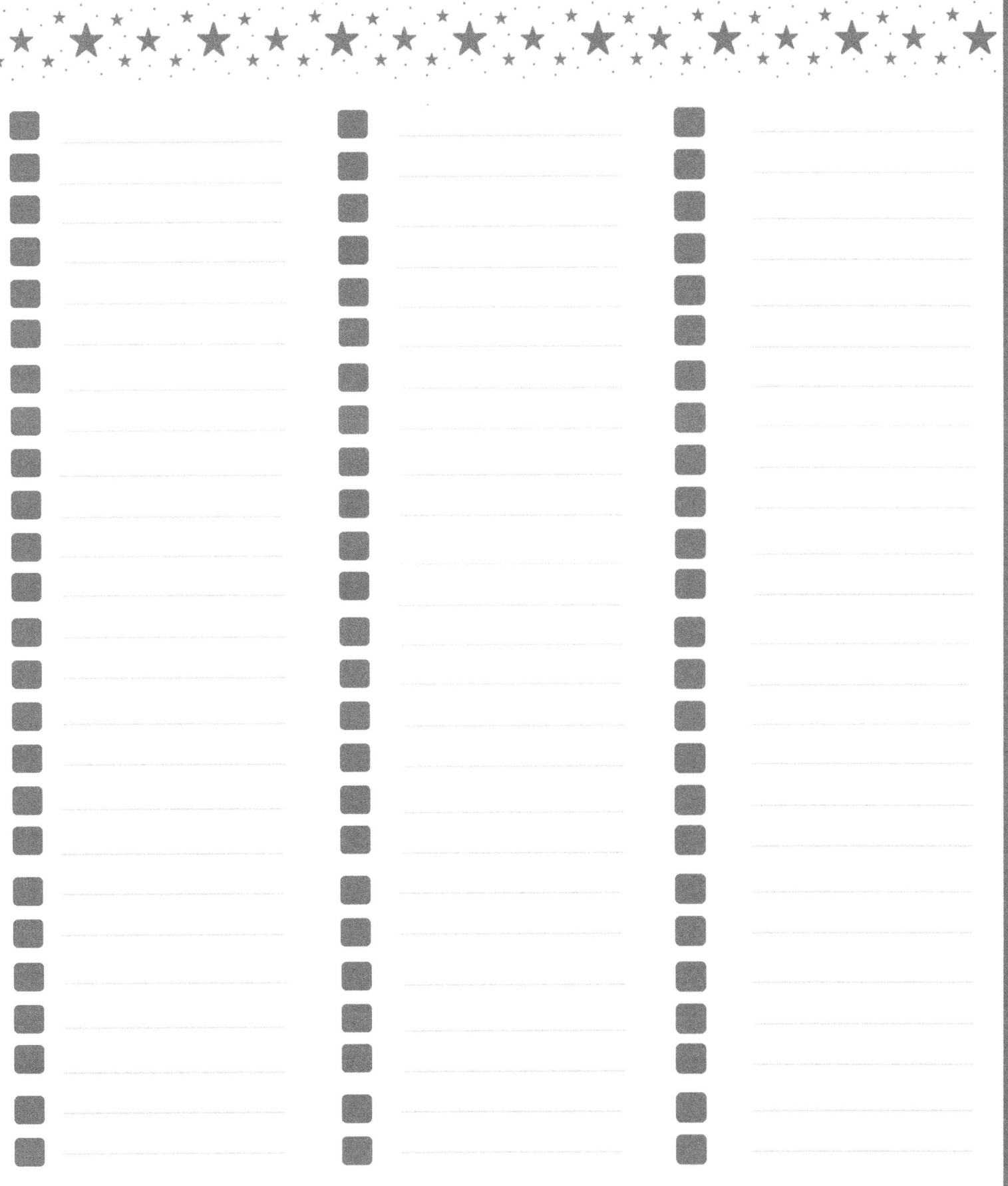

CHRISTMAS GIFT *Ideas*

NAME: **BUDGET:**

GIFT IDEAS

NAME: **BUDGET:**

GIFT IDEAS

NAME: **BUDGET:**

GIFT IDEAS

NAME: **BUDGET:**

GIFT IDEAS

NOTES

CHRISTMAS PARTY *Planner*

| LOCATION | | DATE | |

THEME	DRESS CODE	NOTES

SCHEDULE

TO DO LIST

ACTIVITIES / IDEAS

MEAL PLANNER

HOLIDAY WEEK Schedule

MON	
TUE	
WED	
THU	
FRI	
SAT	
SUN	

PRIORITIES

TO DO

NOTES

Décor PLANNER

THEME

BUDGET　　**ACTUAL COST**

IDEAS

SCHEDULE

COLOR SCHEME

THINGS TO BUY

NOTES

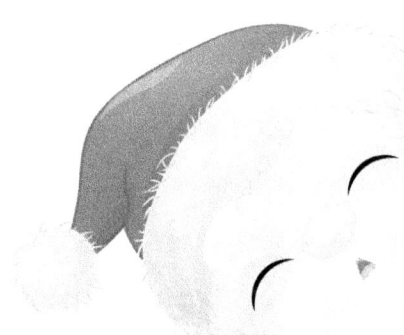

CHRISTMAS SHOPPING *List*

ITEM	PRICE	STORE

NOTES & REMINDERS

CHRISTMAS GIFT Tracker

NAME	GIFT	BOUGHT

CHRISTMAS CARD *Tracker*

RECIPIENT:

ADDRESS:

○ WRITTEN   ○ MAILED   ○ RECEIVED

RECIPIENT:

ADDRESS:

○ WRITTEN   ○ MAILED   ○ RECEIVED

RECIPIENT:

ADDRESS:

○ WRITTEN   ○ MAILED   ○ RECEIVED

RECIPIENT:

ADDRESS:

○ WRITTEN   ○ MAILED   ○ RECEIVED

RECIPIENT:

ADDRESS:

○ WRITTEN   ○ MAILED   ○ RECEIVED

CHRISTMAS PARTY *Invites*

NAME	CONTACT INFORMATION	RSVP'D

CHRISTMAS BUDGET *Tracker*

TOTAL BUDGET GOAL

ACTUAL COST

NAME	BUDGET	GIFT PURCHASED	AMOUNT SPENT

CHRISTMAS GIFT *Tracker*

NAME OF STORE	ITEM TO PURCHASE	COST

ELF ON THE SHELF *Ideas*

SUPPLY LIST

OTHER IDEAS

CHRISTMAS COOKIE Recipe

RECIPE NAME:

Category: **Source:**   **Prep Time:**

Temperature: **Cook Time:**   **Serves:**

INGREDIENTS

DIRECTIONS

NOTES

HOLIDAY *Recipes*

SERVES: **PREP TIME:** **BAKE TIME:**

Ingredients

Instructions

CHRISTMAS *Journal*

CHRISTMAS *Journal*